Teacher's Guide

THE NORTHERN EUROPEAN RENAISSANCE

by Marilyn Chase
Illustrated by Helen Hausner and Larry Weaver

CONTENTS

Indicates full-color transparencies

Note: The answers to all study units will be found at the end of this teacher's guide.

TO THE TEACHER:

This book represents an exciting new development in the world of education. The book contains 12 prepared full-color transparencies which are perforated for easy removal. Reproducibles are included for either testing or additional student exercises.

The proper name spellings in this book are those which coincide with the majority of secondary textbooks extant at this time. It is recommended that the names of persons and places be written on the blackboard as they are discussed.

By way of stimulating more student interest and increasing opportunities for advanced study, these transparencies can be hung, after viewing, against a white background on a classroom bulletin board.

The illustrations in these transparencies are not drawn to scale or for spacial accuracy.

MILLIKEN PUBLISHING CO.

TRANSPARENCES

*Page 1 — HUMANISTS OF NORTHERN EUROPE

BACKGROUND INFORMATION: In northern Europe the ideas and traditions of the Middle Ages died more slowly than in Italy. The new economic and social developments did not cross the Alps until one hundred years after Petrarch and Boccaccio had spread the ideas of ancient Greece and Rome in Italy. There was in northern Europe a preoccupation with religion, and so, when the north turned to the writings of ancient Greece and Rome, they read not only the pagan writers but also the early Christian writers. Humanists of the north revolted against the abuses of the medieval Church but they remained Christian with a deep moral commitment to making life more human and livable in this world. They turned from the medieval emphasis on philosophy and theology to rediscover the simple and pure religion of the early Christian church. They studied the writings of the early Church fathers and began to read the Bible in its original language. This necessitated a full scholarly knowledge of Greek and Hebrew as well as Latin.

By far the most influential of all the Christian humanists was Desiderius Erasmus of Rotterdam. He, more than anyone else, popularized the reform program of Christian humanism. He was born in Holland in 1469, educated by monks, and entered the monastery at an early age. He became dissatisfied with monastic life, however, and left the monastery to begin a life of travel and teaching that took him to France, England, Italy, Germany, and Switzerland. Until he was thirty, Erasmus spent all of his time in studying classical literature. It was not until his first visit to England in 1499 when he met Thomas More that he turned seriously to the religious studies that were to occupy his time for the rest of his life.

The chief aim of Erasmus' work was to restore Christianity to its early simplicity as taught by Christ and his disciples. He believed that Christianity was a way of life and not a system of doctrines and dogmas. In order to understand the original meaning of Christianity he thought it was necessary to go back to the earliest Greek manuscripts of the New Testament. He therefore edited the Greek text of the New Testament and finally, in 1516, after years of work, he published the New Testament in its original Greek. This was the first time the New Testament had been printed in its original language.

Erasmus also worked for the reform of certain practices which he felt were not in harmony with the Christian spirit. He openly criticized the abuses he found in the church. His best known work in this field is the *Praise of Folly,* in which he ridiculed the wealth and power of the clergy and the monastic orders, as well as practices such as pilgrimages, fasts, and the veneration of relics. Because of his wit and humor and his easy, graceful Latin style, he was called the "Prince of the Humanists." Everything he wrote was widely read and he helped to prepare the way for the Reformation.

Thomas More was a Christian humanist from England. He was a scholar, politician, and statesman. He wrote a book, *Utopia,* which was a brilliant criticism of the practices and thinking of his own day. *Utopia* was a vision of a nation at peace with itself and its neighbors. Here was a land where men worked freely for the common good and received what they needed for a comfortable life. There was no slavery, no oppression of the weak by the strong, no ruthless power or wealth concentrated in the hands of a few.

Sir Thomas More achieved the highest political position open to a politician in England. He became Chancellor of England under King Henry VIII, but was later executed when he would not agree to the Act of Supremacy that made Henry the head of the Catholic church in England.

*Page 2 — JOHANN GUTENBERG

BACKGROUND INFORMATION: One of the main reasons for the great outburst of classical learning was the invention of printing. Until the fifteenth century most books had been written by hand and were often inaccurate as well as expensive. These hand-written books took a long time to produce and were very scarce. Some of these manuscripts were very elaborate works of art. Some books were written on expensive cloth and embroidered with jewels, while many were perfumed and dusted with gold or silver. Most people could not afford such costly books.

A few short pamphlets or books had been printed by means of an early printing technique which used wood-cut blocks. An entire page, usually consisting of a few lines of text and a picture, was cut on a single wooden block. This method was expensive, time-consuming, and awkward. The blocks were impractical since they could be used to print only one work and wore out very quickly.

Then, about 1440, Johann Gutenberg of Mainz, Germany, invented movable metal type. This invention made printing practical for the first time and made it possible for men to print copy after copy of a book, easily and quickly. Gutenberg used separate pieces of type which enabled men to print different pages of a book by using the same pieces of type over and over again. Gutenberg used his metal type in combination with two other methods still used today. These were the printing press and sticky ink which is necessary in printing on paper from metal.

The pieces of movable metal type were arranged to form words in even lines and then locked together to make up a unit, which might contain several pages of a book. The entire unit could then easily be placed on the press. After printing, the unit was removed and the types separated to be used again and again for other pages.

In the 1450's Gutenberg published his famous 42-line Bible, so-called because each column contained 42 lines of type. The publication of this Bible marked the beginning of the history of the modern book.

*Page 3 — MARTIN LUTHER

BACKGROUND INFORMATION: In Germany in the early 16th century, many people were dissatisfied with their religious life. The abuses in the Church, evident for two hundred years, needed reforming. The wealth and political power of the Church, the special law courts, the ignorance and immorality of some of the clergy, all served to arouse a strong feeling of discontent with the Church, particularly when the Church demanded money for all types of causes. Many people criticized the doctrines and dogmas of the Church which they believed to be outdated. The rising middle class tended to resent the necessity of priests and sacraments to insure salvation. The rulers of the rising nations of northern Europe also resented the interference of the Pope in national affairs and the payment of taxes to a man they came to regard as a foreign prince. The opportunity to confiscate Church lands and keep tax money in their own countries brought many rulers to side with the reformers. Finally, the intellectual basis for the revolt against the Church came from the humanists. The humanists ridiculed relics, pilgrimages, monks, and the power of the pope on the grounds that these things were not a part of the original Christianity. The man who united all the critics and showed them the way to a new religious experience was Martin Luther.

Martin Luther was born in Germany in 1483 of peasant parents. He was given an excellent education at the University of Erfurt, where he studied law. In 1506 he left the University and became an Augustinian monk. He was ordained a priest and sent to teach at the University of Wittenberg. While at Wittenberg he began to question his beliefs and to criticize the more obvious abuses in the Church. The practice that first aroused him to public protest was that represented by a papal indulgence proclaimed by Pope Leo X to obtain money for the building of St. Peter's basilica in Rome. In Germany, the archbishop of Mainz sent Johann Tetzel to persuade the people to give generously. In his enthusiasm Tetzel claimed that the purchase of an indulgence could bring pardon of sins and even affect sins not yet committed. The Church had never taught that indulgences would take away sin; they were merely a final proof that the sinner was contrite and wished for forgiveness for his sins.

Luther protested against Tetzel's tactics by posting ninety-five theses or propositions on the subject of indulgences on the church door at Wittenberg in 1517. This was the standard practice of the day to announce one's willingness to debate a topic. At Leipzig in 1519, Luther met Johann Eck in public debate. Instead of discussing indulgences, the debate centered around the question of whether Luther would accept the Pope's authority as final in all matters. Luther said that he would accept the teachings of the Bible as the final authority, but not the Pope or even Church councils. This brought him into direct and open conflict with the Pope.

Luther continued to develop his teachings and beliefs. He even called upon the nobility of Germany to unite and destroy the power of the Pope in their states. Finally in 1519, Pope Leo X issued a papal bull (a formal document issued by the Pope) excommunicating Luther. When Luther received the bull, he burned it in the public square at Erfurst, showing that he no longer considered that the Pope had any authority over him. It was not until 1529 that Luther was formally summoned by the civil authority to answer for his rebellion. The Emperor Charles V called the Diet of Worms to decide the case against Luther. (A diet is a formal assembly called to discuss or act upon state or public affairs.) The Diet, after much debate, found Luther guilty of heresy and asked him to recant. He refused with the words: "Here I stand, I cannot do otherwise. God help me. Amen." After this trial, he was declared an outlaw of the empire, but he found shelter in Saxony with Duke Frederick. During his year in enforced leisure, he translated the New Testament into German and began to make plans for organizing a church of his own.

*Page 4 — MARTIN LUTHER'S BELIEFS AND ACCOMPLISHMENTS

BACKGROUND INFORMATION: Luther's beliefs became the doctrine of a new church which came to be called the Lutheran Church. Martin Luther had been concerned all of his life with the very important question of what a man had to do in order to gain salvation. As a young monk he had developed the conception of God as a stern and unforgiving judge, and he had accepted the teaching of the Roman Catholic Church that salvation depended upon "good works" and receiving the sacraments. He spent much time in prayer and fasting in order to convince himself that he had merited salvation. But he still doubted. Then in 1515, after reading St. Paul's Epistle to the Romans, he found his answer. This epistle contained the phrase, "the just shall live by faith." This phrase became the central belief of the Lutheran church. Man could achieve salvation by faith alone. Good works, fasts, and sacraments were unnecessary, and no man needed the services of a pope or a priest for his salvation. A person could find in the Bible those things which he must believe.

As the Lutheran Church finally took shape, it retained a good deal of the old Catholic doctrine and practice. There were, however, changes of vital importance. All the sacraments except baptism and the Lord's Supper were abolished. During the Lord's Supper, Lutherans were allowed to receive both the bread and wine. Infant baptism was retained as an initiation ritual into the Christian community. Monastic orders were completely dissolved. Since the clergy were no longer thought to have special powers, they were permitted to marry and live the life of ordinary men. Luther himself married Katherine von Bora, a former nun, in 1525 and had six children.

Since the Bible played an important role in the new religion, Martin Luther translated it from Latin to German so that more people could read it. The New Testament was translated into German in 1521 and the Old Testament was completed in 1532. The importance of this German Bible can scarcely be overestimated. Luther was a master of German, and his Bible had almost as much influence on the development of the German language as on German religion.

Martin Luther also wrote many hymns in his attempt to reform and simplify public worship. He introduced the idea of the entire congregation joining in the singing of songs during the services. In 1524 he brought out a hymnbook with twenty-three hymns he had written. One of Luther's hymns, *A Mighty Fortress,* became the great battle hymn of the Reformation.

*Page 5 — ELIZABETH I, RENAISSANCE QUEEN

BACKGROUND INFORMATION: On November 17, 1558, Elizabeth Tudor became Queen of England. The daughter of King Henry VIII and Ann Boleyn, she was to rule England for fifty-five glorious years. She was her father's daughter, athletic, red-haired, autocratic, inordinately vain and majestic. She was truly a Renaissance figure thriving on compliments, professions of adoration and gifts. She had a passion for sumptuous clothes and costly jewelry. She wore a different dress almost every day; when she died she left some 2000 dresses and a treasure of jewels. She was witty, sarcastic, coarse, vulgar, bawdy, and extroverted. She was intelligent, and well-educated. She had a marvelous memory, kept meticulous notes, and enjoyed accumulating money.

Queen Elizabeth never married, but she chose men of wit and intelligence for her advisors and men of adventure for her friends and lovers. The only man she ever considered seriously as a husband was Robert Dudley. Dudley was Elizabeth's master of the horse and an old friend from her childhood. Dudley was married, but gossip soon spread that Elizabeth was only waiting for Dudley's wife to die in order to marry him. In 1560, Dudley's wife fell down a flight of stairs and broke her neck. The inquest decided her death was an accident. Dudley's household hinted

suicide, and the world whispered murder. The scandal shook the foundations of Elizabeth's throne. After much deliberation, the queen decided against marriage to Dudley, preferring to remain queen rather than expose herself to the criticism and hostility her marriage to him would cause. In the final analysis Elizabeth really did not want to share her crown or throne with any man; secondly, no man in the Elizabethan Age would have settled for a position secondary to that of his wife.

Elizabeth's most capable councilor was William Cecil. Cecil became First Secretary and later Lord Treasurer of England. With Cecil's advice and direction, Elizabeth settled the religious problem that had plagued England since her father's day. She established the Church of England or Anglican Church. The doctrine of this church was a compromise between the Roman Catholic beliefs and extreme Protestant beliefs. The Anglicans kept many of the ceremonies of the Roman Catholic Church, as well as the organization of the church under bishops and archbishops, but the Queen, rather than the Pope, was recognized as the head of the church.

Throughout her life, Elizabeth encouraged suitors. She enjoyed the gifts she received, but she also enjoyed the political benefits she reaped in keeping royal suitors waiting for her answer. She kept Phillip II of Spain dangling for years with the promise of marriage and an alliance with England. When she believed England was strong enough to withstand Spanish threats, she dropped Philip.

Elizabeth also admired adventurous men. Seamen, explorers, and pirates were welcome at her court. She encouraged the great English sailor, Francis Drake, in his imaginative exploits against the Spanish colonies and galleons. Sir Walter Raleigh was given land in the New World and was encouraged by Queen Elizabeth to send colonists there. Due to her trust and confidence in men like Drake, the English navy grew powerful, and the English treasury grew rich.

*Page 6 — ELIZABETHAN ENGLAND

BACKGROUND INFORMATION: The Renaissance was the great age of social and economic advancement for the middle classes throughout Europe. In England, during the reign of Queen Elizabeth I, the merchants, bankers, yeoman farmers, and highly skilled artisans prospered as the nation grew wealthy and strong during a relatively peaceful era. The old rigid class structures were slowly replaced by a more fluid social structure; merit replaced birth as the criterion for success and promotion; great houses were built; and a real national pride flourished.

The English yeoman had always been considered the backbone of the English economy. Legally a yeoman was anyone who derived an annual income of at least forty shillings from freehold land. During the Middle Ages he had gained his freedom and his own land. Through hard work and conservative investment and saving, he advanced his position, until in the sixteenth century, he had acquired considerable wealth and social position. He lived a pleasant life in the country and spent most of his time outdoors supervising his farm laborers, or hunting, hawking, or fishing in order to add variety to his diet of bread, mutton, and ale.

The commercial classes prospered during Queen Elizabeth's reign. Many fortunes had been accumulated during the reign of Henry VIII when loyalty to the crown had been rewarded with deeds of land taken from the monasteries and disloyal feudal lords. But most merchants and businessmen preferred living in London to residing on country estates. In 1585, London, with 250,000 inhabitants, was the largest city in Europe, its most important trade and banking center, and perhaps the most exciting place on earth. Despite the dirt and physical dangers, there was an endlessly variety of opportunity and acquaintance, scenery, and entertainment. The center of the city's busy life was London Bridge, which the citizens considered "the glory of London." Structures along its sides made it a shopping and dwelling place as well as one of England's main thoroughfares.

Because of the availability of money, many new types of architecture were introduced into England. The manor house was no longer thought of as a fortress but as a home of beauty and comfort. Lighter, more graceful dwellings were constructed from brick or timber and plaster. The black and white half-timbered house became a common sight in the Elizabethan landscape. Little Moreton Hall was the country home of a gentleman and is considered an outstanding example of half-timbered construction.

Longleat was designed and built in 1568 by Sir John Thynne who had bought the estate for 53 pounds in 1540. He boldly built the first classical country house in England, using row upon row of mullioned windows. Sculpture and rich hangings adorned his house. In 1574 Queen Elizabeth visited Longleat and was so impressed with the house that she spent the entire summer there.

*Page 7 — ELIZABETHAN DRAMA

BACKGROUND INFORMATION: The exuberance and intensity of life in Renaissance England found its best expression in the Elizabethan theater, where a mixed company of actors, scholars, and writers reinvented a language and used it to create a literature of great richness, variety, and power. Using blank verse, such men as Marlowe, Jonson, Beaumont, Fletcher, and Shakespeare transformed a medieval theater of stilted morality and mystery plays into a theater that expressed the bawdy and often bloody excesses of an intensely human and individualistic age.

The great period of English drama is often called the age of Shakespeare. William Shakespeare came to London in 1587 from his native town of Stratford. He was a glovemaker's son with little formal education. Soon after his arrival in London, he drifted into theater work, probably as an actor, then as a full fledged playwright. By 1592 he was a well-known dramatist and even wrote plays such as *The Merry Wives of Windsor* at the queen's command. In the course of his career, Shakespeare wrote dozens of plays, thirty-eight of which survive, and became quite a wealthy man.

The Elizabethan playwrights wrote for tough audiences. Their plays were written quickly and filled with action. Dramatists were more concerned with development of character, good imagery, puns, and byplay than with elaborate story lines and plots. Most of them literally begged, borrowed, or stole their plots wherever they could find them. Even Shakespeare was not above taking plots from earlier sources, such as Holinshed's *Chronicles of England, Scotland, and Ireland.*

Physically, the Elizabethan theater was modeled along the lines of the uncovered innyards in which the early travelling actors had performed. Located in the London suburbs because they were illegal in the city itself, firetrap playhouses like the Globe, the Curtain, and the Swan flew flags to announce performances and attracted rowdy, loud, and highly critical audiences. Loafers, fops, truant apprentices, courtiers, and women of questionable virtue came to see the plays and to be seen themselves.

The stage itself was no more than a wooden platform projecting into the pit or arena where the poorer playgoers crowded together, standing and exposed to the weather. The wealthier patrons occupied seats around the stage or directly behind the stage. Costumes were elaborate, but few props were used and audiences were called upon to use their imaginations. There were no actresses, so young boys played all feminine roles.

*Page 8 — POOR PEOPLE OF THE RENAISSANCE

BACKGROUND INFORMATION: The lower classes of society did not share in the general prosperity that the middle class merchants and bankers enjoyed during the Renaissance. In fact, the number of poor people grew in both England and Germany during the sixteenth century. Farm workers, laborers, and small manufacturers were victims of a severe price inflation. In England, larger landholders and land speculators bought up vast tracts of arable land and turned them to pasture land for immense flocks of sheep. As a result, thousands of farmers were turned off the land and forced to move to the cities. Great numbers of people lived in one room in high rise tenements.

Many were unskilled and unemployable, and food prices rose due to a shortage of farm products.

In Germany, the peasant suffered terrible hardships. Most peasants were not allowed to fish or cut timber on the lord's land, while on the other hand, their few crops could easily be destroyed by the upper classes during a hunt. In 1525, the peasants joined with the poor city workers in a revolt against existing social conditions. The revolt was put down with appalling savagery, and the peasants and artisans sank back into a hopeless state of economic slavery.

Beggars were a common sight; hundreds appeared at noble funerals hoping for the alms that were generally given them on such occasions. A good many beggars also doubled as thieves; robbers, purse snatchers, and pickpockets preyed upon everyone. There were so many thieves and robbers in England that few people travelled alone in the country except in the middle of the day, and even fewer people went about in the towns at night.

Underworld "schools" for pickpockets and crooked gamblers had more applicants than they could accept. Books were written describing the men and women who called themselves "conny catchers," that is, cheats, vagabonds, and crooks of all kinds. "Conny catchers" had their own language and various types of tricks with which to "cozen" or cheat the unwary. Card sharping and hooking at windows were the favorite pursuits of criminals.

Every town and city paid men to serve as watchmen, but generally their pay was so inadequate that they did not overexert themselves to catch the thieves. Many times they actually aided the criminals for a share of the loot.

Law-abiding citizens reacted in two ways. They passed more laws and harsher ones; some two hundred crimes warranted a death penalty in England during the sixteenth century. The severed heads of criminals could be seen on spikes atop London bridge, and the swaying bodies on gallows served as a constant reminder that crime did not pay. Another reaction was an attempt to help poor people so that they did not need to turn to crime to live. Laws to aid the poor were passed requiring each county in England to provide work for the able-bodied. Hospitals and schools were built and shelters opened for the unemployable. Many men were put to work as rat catchers in the overcrowded cities.

*Page 9 — FRANCIS I, RENAISSANCE KING

BACKGROUND INFORMATION: Francis I was the embodiment of the ideal Renaissance gentleman. Vigorous, sensual, generous, and cultivated, he was a most illustrious successor to Charlemagne and Louis IX. The king's court became the center of ideas, fashions, and the arts. Whenever the king moved from Paris to one of his many palaces along the Loire river, a train of 12,000 horses was needed to carry the tents, baggage, tapestries, and gold and silver plates that the king owned. Francis surrounded himself with intelligent councilors, witty friends, and beautiful women. He once said that a court without ladies was similar to a springtime without roses. His court was alive with men and women dressed in beautiful clothing, enjoying music, games, revels, and love affairs. His court was especially hospitable to poets and artists, for the king enjoyed poetry and collected beautiful art objects. Francis I was curious, he read good literature, and enjoyed talking to men of learning who came to his court. All subjects were discussed at the king's table from warfare to painting, and the king could discuss all subjects intelligently.

French culture flourished during his reign. He founded royal readerships which developed into the College de France, supported and protected William Bude, an outstanding humanist, and employed Benvenuto Cellini to make beautiful art objects and decorate his palaces. He also enjoyed playing the role of supreme patron and relaxing among a circle of cultured friends. The king spent many hours listening to the humanist scholar, Antoine Macault, reading from his translation of the Greek historian Diodorus. This was the image that he wished transmitted to posterity.

Politically the king was not too successful. Power was often in irresponsible hands, money was spent on ostentatious displays, and offices were distributed according to the whims of pretty women rather than on merit. Early in his reign, Francis met with another impressive Renaissance ruler, Henry VIII of England. Francis tried to persuade Henry to throw his support to France against the Emperor Charles V of Spain and the Empire. He received Henry in a city composed of tents woven with gold thread and arranged festivities that lasted for three weeks. Henry decided to choose the Emperor as his ally because the latter controlled Flanders and the English merchants needed that market for their woolen cloth. Throughout his reign, Francis's foreign policy remained confused, but this was overlooked by most Frenchmen because of the beauty Francis brought to French life.

*Page 10 — CHATEAUX OF FRANCE

BACKGROUND INFORMATION: Francis I was particularly obsessed with constructing castles and palaces for himself in the Loire river valley. In 1519 he ordered the construction of Chambord and the building of this chateau became the real passion of his life. Even when the treasury was empty, and the king had no money to pay the ransoms for his two sons to Spain, or when he was forced to raid the treasuries of his churches, or melt down his subjects' silver, work at Chambord went on steadily.

Chambord is the largest chateau built in the Loire Valley. It is 170 yards long and 128 yards wide and contains 440 rooms. It stands at the end of a long avenue surrounded by 13,600 acres of parkland. A wall twenty miles long surrounds the park. The park was a marvellous place for falconry, hunting, and netting. The goshawk mews of Chambord contained 300 birds, and hundreds of hunting dogs were kept in the kennels. The plan of Chambord is basically feudal with a central keep, four towers, and a wall. The rest of the building, however, was inspired by the Renaissance. The imposing facade has the keep in the center, and is joined to the corner towers of the walls by two story galleries supported by arcades. The terrace or roof of the chateau is a unique spectacle of gables, dormer windows, 800 hundred capitals, 365 chimneys, spires, and bell turrets. All were carved with the sculptor's chisel. From the terrace, the courtiers would watch the start and return of the hunts, military reviews, festivals, and tournaments.

The staircase of Chambord is the most unique ever constructed. It consists of two spirals which are superimposed on each other but do not meet. The center well is open so that one can see from one spiral to the other. In all, the chateau has fourteen large staircases and sixty smaller ones.

The chateau of Chenonceaux came into the possession of Francis when its owner, Thomas Bohier, collector of taxes, died and was found to owe a large sum of money to the French treasury. To pay the debt, Bohier's heirs gave the chateau to the king. The chateau built between 1512-1524 consists of a rectangular mansion with turrets or towers at the corners. It stands on two piers resting on the riverbed. A two-storied gallery stands on the bridge over the river. The gallery is built in a simple, classical Renaissance style which is in marked contrast to the more elaborately decorated older part.

The interior of the chateau contains tiled floors, sixteenth century Flemish tapestries, and fireplaces carved by Jean Goujon.

Chenonceaux has been called the "Chateau of Six Women" because of the part its hostesses have played in its history for four hundred years. Catherine Briconnet, the first owner's wife, supervised the construction, and at her request, many innovations were incorporated into the building to make housekeeping easier. Rooms were placed on either side of a central hall and a straight-flighted staircase was built rather than a spiral.

When Henry II became king in 1547, he gave the chateau to his mistress, Diane de Poitiers. Diane, a widow who always wore mourning clothing of black and white, ordered the construction of a garden and had a bridge built between the chateau and the farther bank.

Queen Catherine de Medici, the King's widow and Regent, forced Diane to give up the chateau when Henry died. Catherine remodeled the chateau by adding the gallery above the bridge. Catherine's daughter-in-law, Louise of Lorraine, inherited the chateau after her husband was assassinated. She retired to the chateau, put on white mourning which she wore to the end of her life, and decorated her bedroom, bed, carpets, and chairs with black velvet.

In the eighteenth century, Madame Dupin became the owner of Chenonceaux. She was famous for the salon she established at Chenonceaux where the leading authors and scholars visited. Jean Jacques Rousseau was tutor to her sons and spent a number of years living at Chenonceaux.

In 1864 Madame Pelouze bought the chateau and restored it to its former beauty.

*Page 11 — ELEGANT DINING OF THE RENAISSANCE

BACKGROUND INFORMATION: In studying and imitating the classical world of Rome, the men of the Renaissance also rediscovered the pleasure that comes with eating food that has been well-prepared and elegantly displayed. The Italians were the first to win a reputation for their elegant tables and exquisite cooking, but the French soon surpassed them due to the efforts of an Italian girl who became Queen of France in the sixteenth century.

Catherine de Medici, daughter of Lorenzo de Medici, came to France in 1532 as the child-bride of Henry II. Catherine was a very feminine and worldly transmitter of the classical manners and modes of Florence, Italy. Trained at the papal court of her uncle, she brought the sophisticated manners of Italy to the French court, along with a small army of Italian chefs to prepare her food. Her cooks introduced to the noble tables of France such eating refinements as artichoke hearts, sweetbreads, truffles, grated Parmesan cheese, liver, and a taste for veal. Encouraged by Catherine, the cooks of France soon created new confections such as macaroons, custard cakes, and "iced cream." Imported for the French table were fine works of Venetian glassware, embroidered tablecloths and napkins, and table silver designed by artists such as Benvenutto Cellini. Also from Italy came that new tool of the cultivated, the fork, though its use north of the Alps remained rare until the seventeenth century.

Catherine was both a gourmet and a glutton. She never worried about her figure or her weight, but gave herself completely to the pleasures of eating well. Catherine's chefs achieved the supreme culinary feat when they prepared a banquet to celebrate the wedding of Catherine's son, Charles IX, to Elizabeth of Austria. The appointed day was a Friday. Since fast had to be observed, no meat could be served. The royal party and hundreds of courtiers were served two barrels of oysters, fifty pounds of whale meat, two hundred crayfish, twenty-eight salmon, ten turbot, eighteen brill, four hundred herring, fifty carp, platters of broiled lobsters, mussels, eighteen trout, and one thousand pairs of frog legs. By 1600 the Parisian chefs were recognized as superior to the masters of cooking in Italy.

The banquet table shown in the transparency contains table pieces from France, Italy, and England. The plates are glazed earthenware from central Italy, the enameled gold figures were executed by Cellini for Francis I and represent Land and Sea, allegorical sources of the precious pepper and salt contained within; the tankard was made for a chamberlain of Henry VIII of striped Venetian glass with a silver gilt mounting of English workmanship; the forks are of Italian wormanship with bird's bills as tines.

*Page 12 — SCIENCE AND SCIENTISTS OF NORTHERN EUROPE

BACKGROUND INFORMATION: Genuine science did not begin with the humanists, who were in general uninterested in observing the physical world. Yet they were interested in anything written in the Roman or Greek era. Therefore they corrected and published all the works of the ancient scientists that they could find, and in this way they gave impetus to scientific thought.

Renaissance artists, engineers, technicians, and inventors also spurred the development of scientific thought because they carried on practical experiments in an effort to solve their professional problems.

German mathematicians and geographers quickly assumed the leadership of the scientific movement in the sixteenth century. The first globe of the earth ever manufactured was the work of Martin Behaim of Nuremberg. It was commissioned in 1492 by the Nuremberg city council and utilized all available geographical knowledge. Since Columbus had not returned from his voyage of discovery, the New World does not appear on it. Mathematicians developed the astroblabe, a navigational instrument for co-ordinating the time of day with the angle of the stars and therefore calculating position. The one shown was made by Regiomontanus, humanist and Arabic scholar of Königsberg, Germany.

The essential factor in the scientific revolution is that the new science abandoned the search for unmeasurable qualities and concentrated attention on quantities and measurable forces and then expressed its laws in mathematical terms. The first great discovery of the sixteenth century was the Copernican hypothesis that revolutionized astronomy. Nicholas Copernicus (1473-1543) was a Polish scholar of wide intellectual interests. He studied medicine, mathematics, astronomy, and church law. Just before his death in 1543, he published a book entitled *Concerning the Revolutions of the Heavenly Bodies.* In his

book, Copernicus, using pure mathematics, stated the hypothesis that the sun is the center of the universe, about which all the planets, including the earth, revolve and that the apparent revolution of the whole system about the earth is actually caused by the daily rotation of the earth on its own axis.

With the publication of this heliocentric theory, Copernicus challenged the many scholars who still believed Aristotle's concept of an earth-centered universe. Yet Copernicus did not throw out all of Aristotle's notions because he still clung to the idea that all planetary motions must be circular. It was not until Johann Kepler (1571-1630) produced a mathematical formula to prove that the planets revolved about the sun in an elliptical orbit, and Galileo Galilei (1564-1642) constructed a telescope to actually observe planetary movements, that the Copernican theory was proven conclusively.

ANSWER KEY FOR STUDY UNITS

Study Unit 1A — Identification and Matching

I. Identification

1. A. Sir Thomas More B. In his book *Utopia* he described a simple society where men were at peace with themselves and their neighbors.

2. A. Desiderius Erasmus B. He wrote *Praise of Folly* and translated the Bible into Greek in an attempt to teach people that Christianity was a way of life, not a system of doctrines and dogmas.

II. Matching

1. h	3. f	5. i	7. k	9. b
2. e	4. g	6. j	8. c	10. a

Study Unit 2A — Completion and Short Essay

I. Completion

1. 15th, hand 2. expensive, inaccurate 3. wooden blocks 4. impractical, expensive, time-consuming, wasteful or awkward 5. movable, type 6. the same type could be used over and over again 7. press, ink 8. 42-line Bible 9. The publication of this book marked the beginning of the history of the modern book. 10. 1,000, 30,000

II. Short Essay

Gutenberg's invention raised the intellectual level in Europe; it provided the Humanists with a wider audience for their writing; books were cheaper and more accurate than ever before.

Study Unit 3A — Identification and Short Essay

I. Identification

1. A. Selling Indulgences B. This practice led to Luther's first public protest against an abuse of the Church. 2. A. Burning the Papal Bull B. This act showed that Luther no longer considered that the Pope had authority over him. 3. A. The Hearing at

Worms B. After this hearing, Luther refused to recant and became a declared outlaw of the Empire.

II. Short Essay

1. The Reformation began in Germany because the abuses in the Church were more apparent there than elsewhere; the rising nationalism of the German princes led them to resent the authority of the pope and his right to collect taxes in their lands; the Christian humanists had great influence there.

2. Probably not, because the Renaissance freed men from the old Medieval ways of thinking about themselves and the world and made them more critical of the world in which they lived and the institutions that they supported.

3. Indulgences took away the punishment that was due a sinner after he had confessed his sins and received pardon for them from a priest. The proclamation of an indulgence by Pope Leo X to help pay for St. Peter's Basilica led to the misrepresentation of the indulgence by Johann Tetzel, which in turn led to Luther's protest and the split within the Christian church.

4. Johann Tetzel told people that the indulgence would take sins away that they had committed and also remove sins not yet committed.

5. The ninety-five theses were propositions on the subject of indulgences that Luther posted on the Church door at Wittenberg. He nailed them to the door to announce his willingness to debate this topic.

6. Luther ultimately denied the supreme authority of the Pope and stated that he accepted only the Bible as his final authority.

Study Unit 4A — Multiple Choice

Multiple Choice

1. c	4. d	7. a	10. c	13. b
2. c	5. a	8. b	11. c	14. c
3. b	6. c	9. a	12. a	15. c

Study Unit 5A — Identification and Short Essay

I. Identification

1. A. Francis Drake B. Great seaman who brought wealth and honor to England and to the Queen. 2. A. William Cecil B. First secretary to the Queen and chief advisor who helped her solve the very difficult question of what church to establish in England. 3. A. Robert Dudley B. Probably the only man Queen Elizabeth seriously considered marrying. She gave him up when her proposed marriage to him threatened to topple her from the throne. 4. A. Walter Raleigh B. Great adventurer who tried to set up a colony in the New World. 5. A. Philip II B. King of Spain who wished to marry Queen Elizabeth. She would not consent but kept him waiting for years until she was sure England could withstand the Spanish threat.

II. Short Essay

1. Henry VIII and Anne Boleyn. 2. She was red-haired, athletic, vain, majestic, and autocratic. 3. She enjoyed compliments; she was witty, sarcastic, coarse, vulgar, bawdy, and extroverted, as well as intelligent, well-educated, greedy. 4. a. She did not wish to share her crown with any man; she feared that her marriage to an Englishman would cause trouble; she could find no man in her age who would settle for second position behind the queen. b. and c. Opinion question. Answers will vary. 5. She established the Anglican Church with beliefs that were partly Catholic and partly Protestant.

Study Unit 6A — Identification and Completion

I. Identification

1. A. Moreton Hall B. Half-timbered construction C. It is an outstanding example of a British black and white half-timbered house.

2. A. Longleat B. Classical style C. First classical style house built in England.

II. Completion

1. middle class 2. Merit 3. yeoman 4. forty
5. monasteries 6. London 7. London Bridge
8. shopping 9. fortress, home 10. work, saving.

Study Unit 7A — Multiple Choice

I. Multiple Choice

1. b	4. b	7. b	10. b	13. c
2. c	5. c	8. c	11. a	14. b
3. a	6. a	9. b	12. d	15. c

II. Answers may vary somewhat.

Marlowe	Johnson
Dr. Faustus	*The Alchemist*
Edward the Second	*Valpone*
The Jew of Malta	*Bartholomew Fair*
Tamburlaine the Great	*Catiline*
et al	et al

Shakespeare
Hamlet
Macbeth
King Lear
Romeo and Juliet
Julius Caesar
As You Like It
Midsummer Night's Dream
Merchant of Venice
Henry the Fifth
Othello
et al

2. a. Marlowe — *The Jew of Malta;* Shakespeare — *The Merchant of Venice* b. *The Jew of Malta*

Study Unit 8A — Completion — Discussion

I. Completion

1. prosperity, depression 2. increased 3. pasture, sheep 4. city 5. hunt, timber 6. beggars 7. crime 8. conny catchers 9. watchmen 10. 200 11. poor laws 12. schools and hospitals 13. rat-catchers 14. inflation 15. hunting

II. Discussion

Answers will vary.

Study Unit 9A — Discussion

1. He possessed many of the qualities that were admired during the Renaissance. He was vigorous, sensual, generous, and cultivated. The king's court became the center of ideas, fashions, and the arts.

2. The king's court was alive with men and women dressed in the latest fashions, enjoying music, games, revels, poetry.

3. He founded royal readerships which developed into the College de France, supported and protected William Bude, collected art objects.

4. He considered himself a patron of the arts and an intellectual and cultured man and encouraged artists to show him as such.

5. He spent money on ostentatious displays, and distributed offices to the whims of pretty women rather than by merit because he admired beauty.

6. Henry VIII needed the support of his merchants who in turn wanted the rich markets of Flanders.

7. Answers will vary according to sources used.

Study Unit 10A — Identification and Completion

I. Identification

a. Spiral staircase b. Arcade of Chambord c. Dormer windows of Chenonceaux d. Turrets of Chenonceaux

II. Completion

1. h	3. f	5. c	7. d	9. j
2. i	4. e	6. b	8. g	10. a

Study Unit 11A — Completion

1. Catherine de Medici 2. cooking 3. truffles, artichokes, iced cream 4. Venetian 5. Benvenuto Cellini 6. fork 7. Charles IX and Elizabeth of Austria 8. fish 9. earthenware 10. salt and pepper 11. tankard 12. Parisan, Italian

Study Unit 12A — Identification and True-False

I. Identification

1. A. Copernicus B. The sun was the center of the universe and all the planets revolved about it C. Students should reproduce drawing shown on transparency. 2. A. Astrolabe B. It was a navigational instrument that helped sailors co-ordinate the time of day with the angle of the stars and so determine their position. C. Regiomontanus of Königsberg Germany.

II. True-False

1. F	4. T	7. F	10. F
2. T	5. F	8. T	11. T
3. F	6. T	9. T	12. T

STUDY UNIT NO. 1A

I. DIRECTIONS: A. Identify each man shown below. B. Tell why he can be considered a Christian humanist.

1. A. _____

   B. _____

   _____

   _____

2. A. _____

   B. _____

   _____

   _____

II. MATCHING QUESTIONS: On each blank in Column A write the letter of the item in Column B which is being described.

COLUMN A

1. _____ A book that described the perfect society in which peace and prosperity were common
2. _____ The chief source of learning for Christian humanists
3. _____ A satire ridiculing the wealth and power of the clergy
4. _____ Emphasized reading and editing the writings of ancient Greece and Rome
5. _____ Emphasized reading the works of the early Church to discover the simplicity of it
6. _____ Chief subjects of the Middle Ages
7. _____ Original language of the New Testament
8. _____ Italian humanist who first discovered the writings of the ancient Greeks and Romans
9. _____ Dutch humanist who left the monastery to become a traveling lecturer
10. _____ English humanist who was executed by King Henry VIII

COLUMN B

a. Thomas More

b. Erasmus

c. Petrarch

d. Hebrew

e. Bible

f. *Praise of Folly*

g. Italian humanism

h. *Utopia*

i. Christian humanism

j. Philosophy and Religion

k. Greek

l. Dante

m. Anatomy and Latin

NAME _____ DATE _____

STUDY UNIT NO. 2A

I. DIRECTIONS: Fill in each blank with a word or words which will make the sentence a correct statement.

1. Until the _____ century most books were written by _____.

2. These books were very _____ and often _____.

3. The earliest printing had been done with _____ _____, each of which had an entire page carved on it.

4. This method of printing was _____ because it was _____ _____, _____, and _____.

5. About 1440, Johann Gutenberg invented _____ metal _____.

6. His invention made printing practical for the first time because _____ _____.

7. Gutenberg also used a printing _____ and a sticky _____.

8. In the 1450's Gutenberg published his famous _____.

9. The publication of this book was important because _____ _____.

10. By the end of the 15th century there were more than a _____ well-known printers, and more than _____ editions had been published.

II. SHORT ESSAY: Briefly discuss the effect Gutenberg's invention had on life in western Europe.

_____

_____

_____

_____

_____

_____

_____

_____

III. Use reference books to obtain information concerning other Renaissance printers, especially Aldus Manutius and William Caxton of England. On a separate sheet of paper, write a brief description of their work and tell why each is important in the story of printing.

MILLIKEN PUBLISHING CO.

STUDY UNIT NO. 3A

I. DIRECTIONS: A. Identify each of the following scenes from Luther's life. B. Tell why each was a significant step in Luther's break with the Church.

1. A. _____

   B. _____

   _____

   _____

2. A. _____

   _____

   B. _____

   _____

   _____

3. A. _____

   B. _____

   _____

   _____

II. SHORT ESSAY: Answer each of these fully on a separate sheet of paper.
1. Why did the Reformation begin in Germany?
2. a. Could the Reformation have taken place before the Renaissance?
   b. Give reasons for your answer.
3. a. What were indulgences? b. How did they have an important effect on history?
4. What selling technique of Johann Tetzel caused Luther to publish his ninety-five theses?
5. a. What were the ninety-five theses? b. Why did Luther nail them to the door of the Castle Church?
6. During the Leipzig debate, what position did Luther ultimately assume in his debate with Johann Eck?

THE NORTHERN EUROPEAN RENAISSANCE

3A

MILLIKEN PUBLISHING CO.

STUDY UNIT NO. 4A

MULTIPLE CHOICE. Directions: Select the letter of the correct answer and place it on the blank line.

1. _____ Martin Luther's beliefs became the doctrine of a new church known as the a. Protestant Church b. Presbyterian Church c. Lutheran Church d. Reformed Church.

2. _____ Luther was concerned throughout his life with the question of a. indulgences. b. the Pope's authority. c. how to merit salvation. d. clerical marriages.

3. _____ The Catholic Church taught that man was saved through a. faith in Christ. b. prayer and good works. c. indulgences. d. believing in the Pope's authority.

4. _____ The central teaching of Martin Luther concerning those who were saved was a. all who led good lives. b. only those who received indulgences. c. those who fasted and prayed. d. those who had faith in Jesus Christ.

5. _____ The chief source of authority for Martin Luther was a. The Bible. b. the Pope. c. himself. d. monks, priests, and bishops.

6. _____ Luther's translation of the Bible played an important part in fixing the standards for the a. Greek language. b. Hebrew language. c. German language. d. English language.

7. _____ Luther retained a. two b. seven c. five d. none of the sacraments of the Catholic Church.

8. _____ Luther abolished a. churches. b. monks and monasteries. c. marriages of priests. d. hymns.

9. _____ Luther wrote many hymns and introduced to services a. congregational singing. b. singing by professional choirs. c. children's choirs. d. organ music.

10. _____ The great battle hymn of the Reformation was entitled a. The Battle Hymn of the Republic. b. Faith of Our Fathers. c. A Mighty Fortress is Our God. d. God, Our Bulwark and Our Strength.

11. _____ Luther was excommunicated by Pope a. Clement VII. b. Urban X. c. Leo X. d. Martin V.

12. _____ Luther was declared an outlaw of the empire by a. Charles V. b. John I. c. Leo X. d. Francis I.

13. _____ Luther was trained as a a. doctor b. lawyer c. priest at the University of Erfurt in Germany.

14. _____ Luther left Erfurt to become a a. Franciscan monk. b. Dominican monk. c. Augustinian monk.

15. _____ Luther earned a great reputation as a teacher at a. Erfurt. b. Worms. c. Wittenberg. d. Leipzig.

THE NORTHERN EUROPEAN RENAISSANCE   MILLIKEN PUBLISHING CO.

NAME _____ DATE _____

STUDY UNIT NO. 5A

I. IDENTIFICATION: Directions: Identify each person and tell what part each one played in the life of Queen Elizabeth I.

1. A. _____

   B. _____

   _____

   _____

1.

2. A. _____

   B. _____

   _____

   _____

2.

3. A. _____

   B. _____

   _____

   _____

3.

4. A. _____

   B. _____

   _____

   _____

4.

5. A. _____

   B. _____

   _____

   _____

5.

II. SHORT ESSAY: Answer the following questions about Queen Elizabeth I on a separate sheet of paper.
   1. Who were her father and mother?
   2. Describe her physical appearance.
   3. Describe her personality.
   4. a. Give reasons why Queen Elizabeth never married. b. Do you think her reasons were valid ones? c. Why or why not?
   5. How did she settle the Church problem between Catholics and Protestants?   5A

NAME _____ DATE _____

STUDY UNIT NO. 6A

I. DIRECTIONS: Answer the following questions about each picture.

1. A. Identify this structure.

_____

B. What style of architecture does it represent?

_____

C. Why is it significant?

_____

_____

2. A. Identify this structure _____

B. What style of architecture does it represent? _____

C. Why is it significant? _____

_____

II. Fill in each blank with a word from the list to make a true statement.

1. The _____ _____ grew prosperous during the Renaissance.

2. _____ replaced birth as the criterion for advancement.

3. The _____ has always been considered the backbone of the English economy.

4. Legally a yeoman was anyone who had an annual income of _____ shillings from land.

5. The commercial classes prospered during the Elizabethan era because they had received land taken from the _____ during Henry VIII's reign.

6. _____ was the largest city in Europe and the residence of most English businessmen.

7. _____ _____ was considered the "glory of London".

8. Bridges were used to cross the river but served as _____ centers as well.

9. Changes occurred in architecture when the manor was no longer built as a _____ but as a _____ of beauty and comfort.

10. Most of the middle class advanced their social positions through _____ and _____.

work   middle class   saving   yeoman   fortress   home   London Bridge   Longleat
monasteries   upper class   Tower of London   shopping   forty   London   fifty   merit
money   Paris   peasants

THE NORTHERN EUROPEAN RENAISSANCE

6A

MILLIKEN PUBLISHING CO.

STUDY UNIT NO. 7A

I MULTIPLE CHOICE. Directions: Select the letter of the correct answer and place it on the blank line.

1. _____ The best expression of what life was like in England during the Renaissance is found in a. the poems of Shakespeare. b. the drama of Marlowe, Jonson and Shakespeare. c. morality plays.

2. _____ Elizabethan drama was written in a. narrative form. b. rhymed couplets. c. blank verse.

3. _____ Elizabethan drama was usually a. bloody and bawdy. b. highly moral and intellectual. c. serious and tragic.

4. _____ Leading English dramatists were a. Jonson and Plautus. b. Shakespeare and Marlowe. c. Shakespeare and Byron.

5. _____ Shakespeare was born in a. London. b. Suffolk. c. Stratford.

6. _____ His formal education consisted of a. little or no schooling. b. three years at Oxford University. c. apprentice training as a glovemaker.

7. _____ Shakespeare won fame and popularity in less than a. 10 years. b. 5 years. c. 15 years.

8. _____ Shakespeare wrote a. Hamlet b. Midsummer Night's Dream c. The Merry Wives of Windsor at the request of Queen Elizabeth I.

9. _____ Shakespeare wrote his plays for a. highly intellectual audiences. b. the common man and woman. c. scholars and intellectuals. d. Queen Elizabeth and her court.

10. _____ a. Imagery b. Plots c. Puns were the least important part of a play to the Elizabethan dramatists.

11. _____ Shakespeare "lifted" story lines for his plays from a. Holinshed's Chronicles. b. Medieval Mystery Plays. c. other Elizabethan dramatists.

12. _____ The Swan Theater was modeled according to a. a rectangular floor plan. b. a circular plan. c. a square plan. d. an uncovered innyard.

13. _____ Roles in Elizabethan drama were played by a. men. b. women and men. c. boys and men.

14. _____ a. Costumes b. Props c. Stage effects were few in number in Elizabethan theater.

15. _____ Elizabethan theaters were usually located in the a. city. b. countryside. c. suburbs. d. innyards.

II Use reference books to find the answers to the following questions. Write your answers on a separate sheet of paper.
1. Name the best-known plays of Shakespeare, Marlowe, and Jonson.
2. a. Find out which two plays, one by Shakespeare and one by Marlowe, have similar plots. b. Which of these two plays was written first?

7A

MILLIKEN PUBLISHING CO.

NAME _____ DATE _____

STUDY UNIT NO. 8A

I. DIRECTIONS: Fill in each blank with a word that will make the sentence a correct statement.

1. The Renaissance was a time of _____ for the middle class but one of economic _____ for the lower classes of farm workers and laborers.

2. The number of poor people _____ in England and Germany during the Renaissance.

3. The land speculators bought up large tracts of arable land and turned them into _____ for grazing _____ .

4. Farmers left the land to move to the _____ where they were generally un-employed.

5. Peasants in Germany were still not allowed to _____ or cut _____ on the Lord's land.

6. _____ were a common sight in all towns.

7. _____ usually increased because there were so many poor people un-able to find work.

8. Cheats and crooks were called _____ _____ because they knew all kinds of tricks to cheat the unwary.

9. _____ were hired to patrol the streets.

10. _____ crimes brought the death penalty in England.

11. _____ _____ were passed to help unemployed and unskilled people.

12. Each county had to provide work for the able-bodied and set up _____ and _____ for the poor.

13. Jobs such as _____ were created to give men work.

14. A shortage of farm products caused a serious price _____ which made it very difficult for poor people to live.

15. Many peasants in Germany lost their crops when the upper classes went _____ and rode across their fields.

II. DISCUSSION QUESTION: Answer this question fully on the back of this paper.
   a. Do you favor the establishment of more severe laws to punish law breakers, or do you favor creating programs that will help to eliminate the causes for crime?
   b. Give reasons to support your answer. Look for recent magazine articles to find out what solutions have been proposed in your own country to fight the rising crime rate.

THE NORTHERN EUROPEAN RENAISSANCE

MILLIKEN PUBLISHING CO.

NAME _____ DATE _____

STUDY UNIT NO. 9A

I. DIRECTIONS: Identify each of the following details of Renaissance architecture.

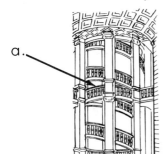

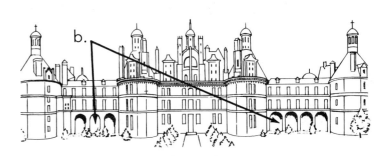

a. _____   b. _____

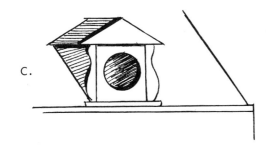

c. _____   d. _____

II. MATCHING: On each blank in Column A write the letter of the item in Column B
that is being described.

Column A

1. _____ He carved fireplaces in Chen-onceaux.

2. _____ Supervised the building of Chenonceaux to see that it was easy to keep up

3. _____ Built Chenonceaux for his wife

4. _____ Gave Chenonceaux to Diane

5. _____ She built the long gallery at Chenonceaux.

6. _____ "Chateau of Six Women"

7. _____ She always wore mourning of black and white.

8. _____ Her bedroom was furnished all in black.

9. _____ She hired Rousseau as a tutor to her sons.

10. _____ Chateau with over 74 staircases

Column B

a. Chambord

b. Chenonceaux

c. Catherine de Medici

d. Diane de Poitiers

e. Henry II

f. Thomas Bohier

g. Louise of Lorraine

h. Jean Gaujon

i. Catherine Briconnet

j. Madam Dupin

k. Madam Pelouze

MILLIKEN PUBLISHING CO

NAME _____ DATE _____

STUDY UNIT NO. 10A

DIRECTIONS: Answer the following questions about the Renaissance in France.

1. Why can Francis I be called an ideal Renaissance gentleman?

_____

_____

_____

2. Describe the king's court.

_____

_____

_____

3. What specific things did Francis I accomplish to help French culture to develop?

_____

_____

_____

4. Why is the picture of Francis listening to a reading of Greek history one that he wanted transmitted to posterity?

_____

_____

_____

5. What were some of the obvious disadvantages of having a king who loved beautiful objects as a ruler?

_____

_____

_____

6. Why did Francis lose the support of Henry VIII? Do you think it was necessary to impress Henry with the city made of cloth of gold?

_____

_____

_____

7. Look up information in other sources and write a few sentences about each of the following persons describing the part they played in the French Renaissance.

Answer on the back of your paper.

Henry II   Diane de Poitiers   Catherine de Medici   Rabelais   Montaigne

STUDY UNIT NO. 11A

DIRECTIONS:

I. Fill in each blank with the word from the list below that will make the sentence a true statement.

1. _____introduced Italian manners and modes of living into France.

2. She was especially interested in the fine art of _____.

3. Various eating refinements such as _____, _____, and _____were introduced into France.

4. _____glassware, embroidered tablecloths, table silver, and gold table decorations were imported from Italy.

5. _____was commissioned to produce silver and gold table decorations.

6. The _____was also introduced as an eating implement for the very refined.

7. The wedding of _____and _____was the occasion for a magnificent banquet.

8. Only _____was served at this magnificent banquet.

9. The dining table contained plates made of _____from Italy.

10. The table decoration showing land and sea contained _____and _____.

11. The _____was made for a chamberlain of Henry VIII of Venetian glass.

12. By the year 1600 _____chefs had surpassed _____master chefs in the preparation of elegant food.

oil and vinegar   forks   china   Florentine   salt and pepper   cooking   fish   truffles tankard   painting   vegetables   artichokes   Parisian   Louise of Lorraine   spoons iced cream   Italian   earthenware   Venetian   hamburger   snails   Henry III Catherine de Medici   Benvenuto Cellini   Charles IX   Elizabeth of Austria.

II. DISCUSSION QUESTION: Discuss these questions fully on the back of this paper. A. Why do you think gourmet eating and elegant preparation of food appeal to people? B. Do you think that people are interested in cooking and eating well today? Explain your answer and give examples.

THE NORTHERN EUROPEAN RENAISSANCE   MILLIKEN PUBLISHING CO.

NAME _____ DATE _____

I. DIRECTIONS: Answer the questions about each picture.

1. A. Who is this? _____

B. What hypothesis did he propose?

_____

_____

C. Illustrate his theory at lower left.

1.

2. A. What instrument is shown on the right?

_____

B. What was its purpose?

_____

_____

C. Who constructed it? _____

_____

2.

II. TRUE OR FALSE: Circle the T if the sentence is true; circle the F if the sentence is false.

1. The Christian humanists began the study of genuine science. T F

2. Artists and engineers were really the first practical scientists of the Renaissance. T F

3. Italian mathematicians and geographers led the way in the development of scientific thought and reasoning. T F

4. The first globe of the earth was made in Germany in 1492. T F

5. The first globe was very accurate and even contained the first outline of the New World. T F

6. The chief characteristic of Renaissance science was its emphasis on measuring and exploring quantities. T F

7. Copernicus stated that the earth was the center of the universe around which the planets revolved. T F

8. Aristotle had first developed the theory of an earth-centered universe. T F

9. Copernicus accepted Aristotle's belief that the earth and other planets moved in circular orbits. T F

10. Kepler invented a telescope to actually prove through experience that the earth was the center of the universe. T F

11. Mathematics was the really important study that made Copernicus' discovery possible. T F

12. Galileo believed Kepler's theory that the planets revolved about the sun in an elliptical orbit. T F

THE NORTHERN EUROPEAN RENAISSANCE

MILLIKEN PUBLISHING CO.

Country life

Similar to middle class
 fishing
women - short sleeves (should have long sleeves)
 usually dress - use for all seasons
 didn't wash
 close quarters -- houses small
 poor hovels

bugs in bed -- due to straw

wooden houses - rushes on floors
 rushes would be filthy
some inside bathrooms (drainage,
 sewage)